EFRAÍN OF THE SONORAN DESERT

A Lizard's Life Among the Seri Indians

By Amalia Astorga,
Seri Indian Elder
As told to Gary Paul Nabhan

Illustrated by Janet K. Miller

AS I PULLED MY KAYAK up onto the beach below the Seri village—before any of the girls and boys ran up to greet me—I spotted a zebra-tailed lizard lounging in the sun. Thirty years have gone by, but that is what I remember from my first time visiting the Seri Indian villages which are situated along the coast of the Sea of Cortez. I recall how fast that lizard ran to get away from me as soon as I splashed onto the shore, its striped tail curled high so as not to get it wet.

I had come back to that Seri village from the islands—across the channel—where their ancestors had lived for centuries. I was eager to learn more about how they survived and prospered in an environment that was as seemingly harsh and dry as the Sonoran Desert.

3

THERE ARE HARDLY MORE THAN 600 Seri Indians alive today, which is why they are sometimes called "endangered people." And yet, they are not doomed with extinction simply because they are so few in number. I will never forget how alive these Seri people are, singing and dancing for me and my friends, trading their beautiful baskets to us in exchange for food, and selling us their wonderful carvings of animals. Their carvings, far from being lifeless, capture the lovely movements of desert and marine animals, which the Seri know better than any other people living in Mexico.

The animal carving I took home with me some 25 years ago looks just like a real-life lizard. It's the same size and shape. It even has the same stance. This particular lizard is endangered, a scientist later told me. "Endangered?" I asked. "Everywhere I looked on that island, there were lizards…" The Seri villages are not the places where lizards are threatened with extinction, the scientist told me. "It's a curious thing," he said, scratching his head, "but there seem to be more lizards around wherever the Seri live."

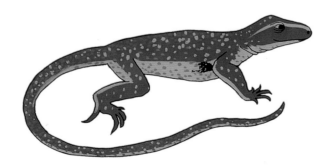

I WONDERED what the scientist meant by that. How could it be that the lizards are rare where Indians once lived, but those same lizards still thrive where the Indians live today? Could it be, I wondered, that the Seri themselves protect lizards some way?

I puzzled over this question for years, until one day I opened a trunk full of old keepsakes from my travels, and there, still as shiny and solid as when I first purchased it, I found my first Seri Indian lizard carving. I held the old carving in my hands, turning it over until I saw on its bottom side the signature of its maker, José Astorga. I decided right then to try to find that man or one of his kin to ask him about his people's secrets for keeping the lizards abundant.

When I arrived once more at the Seri village on the shores of the sea, his neighbors told me that José had died, but then they pointed to another person—his daughter—sitting in the shade of an ancient ironwood tree listening to the breeze rustle its leaves. Her name was Amalia, and she, like her father, was a woodcarver, a plant-gatherer and a storyteller. When I asked her if her people knew anything special which would help us keep lizards from going extinct, she turned to me, and began to weep.

SHE ASKED ME—

"Which kind of lizard are you speaking of?

Each of them has its own name in our native tongue,

and each of them has its own way of living on the desert shores.

I am sorry for my tears. Let me tell you of a special friend.

"His name, as we knew him, was Efraín, a sand-dwelling lizard.
   When I first saw him, he was rising from the sand into the sun
   and turning his head to look at my house,
   as if he were sizing it up. He looked carefully at me.

"I looked at him, too. It was clear: he was not like other lizards.
   He had no tail past this point…" Amalia said, looking down
   and moving her hand side-ways across her thighs,
"He ran around without a tail, something few lizards do.

"I saw him acting like a person, watching me and thinking.
Efraín was even built like a man, stout with strong arms,
thick legs, big neck, strong muscles and bones.
Like a wrestler, a boxer, a football player, that was Efraín.

"He decided he liked me too, right there and then.
For the next seven years, he came to visit every day.
I could count on him coming near my door every morning by eight.
That Efraín, he never failed to show, not even once.

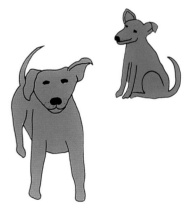

"At first he'd just come, sit beside me and stare out to sea,

   but after some months, he'd let me bounce him on my knee.

   I would bring him dry wheat, which he'd scratch at and eat,

   but I'd never make him do tricks for treats. Still, he grew big with me.

"For the next five months, Efraín would always come alone.
  But then, as the summer grew hot and the desert dried out,
  he started bringing his wife and kids with him to drink.
  I'd put a saucer of water out in the sand, and they would come to lap it up.

"They all came visiting for many years, every day,
  but Efraín remained my favorite. My sister once looked at him and said,
  'He's as true to you as any husband could be.'
  My entire family loved him, the whole village knew him well.

16

"Then one day, while I was out gathering stems from the limberbush
so I could sit with Efraín and make some baskets,
he tried to visit while I was gone. None of my family
saw him at first, which is too bad, because the wild dogs did.

"We have all kinds of dogs in our village, some good, some bad.
We love our Mexican hairless dogs and our floppy-eared mutts,
and we name each one for our ancestors and their ancient camps.
But some dogs dumped out near our village run wild, unnamed.

"He must have tried to escape from them, running hard,
  but they caught him at last by one of his back legs.
  He kept on running toward my home, hiding under my chair,
  but before I had returned, Efraín had died.

"When I arrived back home, I could see that my daughter was crying.
  'What shall we do?' she wailed, holding his limp body in her hand.
  'We must bury him out in the desert,' I said, 'as we would do
  for a great elder, or for a sacred leatherback turtle.' And I wept as well.

"We took him away to a place far beyond the pesky dogs.
 It was quiet. I could only hear my long dress brushing the sand.
 There we dug and dug until we hit the coolest sand, and buried him,
 my daughter Ana making his grave with a cross of cactus wood.

"I cried and cried for many days and couldn't bring myself to eat,
even though my family brought me cactus fruits and fish.
All I could do was remember Efraín, the lizard who made my life so rich.
I was getting thin with sadness my sister said, I missed him so much."

—**AND THAT ENDED** Amalia's story.

The Seri Indians

WANDER DOWN into some of the hottest and driest lands in North America, and you'll come upon a tribe known to outsiders as the Seri Indians. They have lived along the dry coasts of the ocean for centuries, celebrating the animals of the deserts and seas around them. Today, they live along the shores of the Sea of Cortez, also known as the Gulf of California, but they originally came from Baja California, far to the south of the border towns of Calexico and San Diego. Their current homes are some two hundred miles south of the U.S./Mexico border, but they traditionally roamed as far north as the Colorado River delta, just 30 miles south of Arizona and California.

The Seri call themselves the Comcaac, which means the People, although they also consider you and me, leatherback turtles, giant boojum trees and teddy-bear cholla kinds of people as well. Of their people, there are now 650 individuals, far more than at any other time during the last century. The Seri claim they are not close kin to any other Indian tribes living nearby, but are descended from Giants who once lived on the peninsula of Baja California. Scientists agree that the Seri are not closely related to any of the other Native Americans now living in Mexico and the United States, and that their language is also quite unique. Due to diseases introduced by the Spanish and warfare with others who did not understand their lifeways, the Seri tribe once dwindled down to less than 200 individuals who spoke this distinctive language. Even though conditions have recently improved for them, ethnologists still consider the Seri "an endangered people" whose language—so rich in the lore of the Sonoran desert and its animal and plant inhabitants—needs protection from the risk of extinction.

(OPPOSITE) Seri women make beautiful baskets, pottery vessels, shell necklaces and dolls, mostly to sell. The baskets are woven from the fibers of the limberbush, and are woven so tightly, they can hold water. Some five-foot tall baskets are still made today.

You have probably heard about other endangered cultures whose languages are near extinction. Fewer than 8,000 Yanomami survive in the Amazon. If introduced diseases continue to kill off their population, their language and culture will be lost forever. Other rainforest peoples are close to extinction because of the mechanized encroachment on their homelands and the destruction of the diverse habitats that have supplied them for centuries with food and medicine. As these peoples are forced to move away from their original homelands, they are forced to speak other languages and are at risk of losing their own. But other languages of native peoples are endangered well beyond the Amazonian rainforests and the Sonoran desert. Aramaic, an ancient Middle Eastern language that Jesus heard when he was a boy two thousand years ago, is on the verge of extinction. So are many tribal languages in California, Mexico and Australia. As many as 3,500 of the world's remaining 6,500 languages may die this century if no one does anything to ensure that native speakers live in touch with one another in healthy communities and in healthy environments within their homelands.

Fortunately, Seri elders are actively teaching their language and traditions to their children so that language loss will never occur in their homeland. Because the language is fun to speak, with wonderful stories, songs and jokes in it, most Seri children eagerly want to learn it. The Seri language has a rich vocabulary for expressing their knowledge and respect for the many unusual plants and animals that grow on the coast of Mexico and on nearby islands. For example, they give nicknames to animals such as desert tortoises, which they call "the ones who tuck their heads inside," or "the ones who hide beneath trees."

Nearly every Seri child can sing a nursery rhyme about the little horned lizard that lives in the desert near their village, and some children have raised lizard babies to adulthood, feeding them ants and other foods they favor. The Seri name more than 48 kinds of lizards, turtles and snakes of the deserts and seas, and they sing songs and tell stories about many of these.

In a desert where rains are unpredictable, and in seas where currents and whirlpools are treacherous, the Seri often get stranded far from their homes. When such calamities occur,

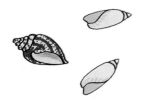

(Opposite) The Seris recycle and use things that wealthier cultures cast off, mixing natural materials rich in Seri tradition with modern industrial man-made ones. The kids will take an old car and use it as if it were a fancy piece of playground equipment.

Chuckwalla ⊙ Ziix Hast Iizx Ano Coom

Long-nosed Leopard Lizard ⊙ Hant Pzl

Desert Side-Blotched Lizard ⊙ Tozipla

Banded Gecko ⊙ Cozixoj

Sonoran Collared Lizard ⊙ Hast Coof

Desert Spiny Lizard ⊙ Aasj

Zebra-Tailed Lizard ⊙ Ctamófi

Regal Horned Lizard ⊙ Hant Cooxoj

the Seri today must rely on their knowledge of desert foods and medicines just as their ancestors did in the past. Several turtles, snakes and iguana-like lizards are still used as survival foods, and 12 kinds of reptiles are used as emergency medicines. Should someone in their family be accidentally bitten by a rattlesnake, Gila monster or sea snake, Seri elders treat these bites with certain medicinal herbs from the desert which reduce swelling, shock and the likelihood of infections. If you were stranded on a remote island with rattlesnakes around you, I'm sure you would welcome the presence of a Seri companion who knew how to use cactus, saltbush, wild oregano and other plants in case of snakebites!

The Seri elders also tell their grandchildren about mythic snakes that live high in the mountains, protecting fresh water springs from anyone who pollutes their water or drinks too much of it. They sing songs whenever they travel between two islands where a giant snake is said to live at the bottom of the treacherous channel. Without singing the songs to calm the snake and the waters which he controls, huge waves can rise up and smash or capsize any boat load of people who fail to show their respect to this creature.

The Seri are now showing their respect for reptiles in other ways. Recently, with the help of the Amazon Conservation Team, the Columbus Zoo, and the Arizona-Sonora Desert Museum, they have begun to raise and breed an endangered chuckwalla known only from Isla San Esteban, an animal which they once ate as food when they lived out on that island. Today, however, the Seri school helps to take care of a half-dozen of these chuckwallas at a time, and hopes to offer their surplus baby chuckwallas to zoos and research institutes making studies to aid in their conservation. After school, both the schoolchildren and their parents gather around the chuckwalla exhibit to sun themselves and to chew on cholla cactus. The ancient stories and songs about chuckwallas have again become a living part of Seri culture, a century after the Seri were forced off Isla San Esteban, or were killed for trying to stay there among the chuckwallas and other native wildlife. By seeing chuckwallas prosper, the Seri community is healing as well.

(*Opposite*) *The Seri name more than 48 kinds of lizards, turtles and snakes of the deserts and seas, and sing songs and tell stories about many of these.*

31

BECAUSE THE SERI HAVE SUCH DETAILED KNOWLEDGE of desert plants and animals, many foreigners have come to the Seri villages to learn survival skills. While the elders do not mind helping these students from other cultures, they are more interested in ensuring that their own grandchildren learn how to survive in the desert and protect the wildlife there. Specially prepared school books, cassette tapes of animal songs, posters, and field trips are all making desert and marine animals a continuing part of Seri culture. If you wish to support these efforts, contact the following places:

Amazon Conservation Team: 2334 Wilson Boulevard; Arlington, VA 22201. 703-522-4684, (fax) 703-522-4464. www.amazonteam.org

Arizona-Sonora Desert Museum: 2021 North Kinney Road; Tucson, AZ 85743. 520-883-1380, (fax) 520-883-2500. www.desertmuseum.org

Center for Sustainable Environments: Northern Arizona University; P.O. Box 5765, Hanley Hall, Flagstaff, AZ 86011-5765. 520-523-6726, (fax) 520-523-8223. www.environment.nau.edu

Many thanks to the Lannon foundation for funding this book and for their continued support.

cinco Puntos Press

Visit us at
www.cincopuntos.com
or call 1-800-566-9072

Cinco Puntos thanks writer Susan Blumenthal and Cecil Dobbs of www.folkart.com for permission to use their text as basis for the description of the Seri found on the dust jacket poster.

Cover design, book design, and typesetting by Vicki Trego Hill of El Paso, Texas.
Printed in Hong Kong by Morris Printing.

Efraín of the Sonoran Desert: A Lizard's Life Among the Seri People. Copyright © 2001 by Amalia Astorga and Gary Paul Nabhan. Illustrations copyright © 2001 by Janet K. Miller. All rights reserved. No part of this book may be used or reproduced in any manner whatsoever without written permission except in case of brief quotations for reviews. For information, write Cinco Puntos Press, 2709 Louisville, El Paso, Texas 79930; or call at 915-566-9072. Printed in Hong Kong.
FIRST EDITION   10   9   8   7   6   5   4   3   2   1
Library of Congress Cataloging-in-Publication Data. Astorga, Amalia. Efrain of the Sonoran Desert : a lizard's life among the Seri people / by Amalia Astorga as told to Gary Paul Nabhan ; illustrated by Janet K. Miller.— 1st ed.   p. cm.   ISBN 0-938317-55-5   1. Seri Indians—Juvenile literature. 2. Lizards—Effect of human beings on—Mexico—Juvenile literature. [1. Seri Indians. 2. Indians of Mexico. 3. Lizards.]   I. Nabhan, Gary Paul. II. Miller, Janet K., 1959-   . ill. III. Title. F1221.S43 A88 2001. 305.8975—dc21   2001028080